Guess Who
Grunts

Dana Meachen Rau

Marshall Cavendish
Benchmark
New York

I live on a farm.

My home is called a pen.

My body is round.

My body is pink.

I have a curly tail.

I have floppy ears.

I have four feet.

They are called *hooves*.

My eyes are small.

I cannot see well.

I smell with my strong *snout*.

I dig with my snout.

I am smart.

I come when you call.

I eat from a *trough*.

I eat corn and scraps.

My babies are called *piglets*.

They drink my milk.

I can be loud.

I oink and grunt.

I roll in the mud.

Mud keeps me cool.

I nap in soft hay.

Who am I?

I am a pig!

Who am I?

eyes

hooves

piglets

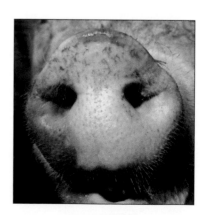

snout

28

tail

trough

Challenge Words

hooves (hoovz) The feet of a pig.

piglets (PIG-lehts) Baby pigs.

snout The flat nose and jaws of a pig.

trough (trawf) A long, open container from which pigs eat.

Index

Page numbers in **boldface** are illustrations.

About the Author

Dana Meachen Rau is the author of many other titles in the Bookworms series, as well as other nonfiction and early reader books. She lives in Burlington, Connecticut, with her husband and two children.

With thanks to the Reading Consultants:

Nanci Vargus, Ed.D., is an Assistant Professor of Elementary Education at the University of Indianapolis.

Beth Walker Gambro is an Adjunct Professor at the University of St. Francis in Joliet, Illinois.

Marshall Cavendish Benchmark
99 White Plains Road
Tarrytown, New York 10591-5502
www.marshallcavendish.us

Library of Congress Cataloging-in-Publication Data

Rau, Dana Meachen, 1971–
Guess who grunts / by Dana Meachen Rau.
p. cm. — (Bookworms. Guess who)
Summary: "Following a guessing game format, this book provides young readers with
clues about a pig's physical characteristics, behaviors, and habitats, challenging readers
to identify it"—Provided by publisher.
Includes index.
ISBN 978-0-7614-2906-7
1. Swine—Juvenile literature. I. Title. II. Series.
SF395.5.R38 2009
636.4—dc22
2007024610

Editor: Christina Gardeski
Publisher: Michelle Bisson
Designer: Virginia Pope
Art Director: Anahid Hamparian

Photo Research by Anne Burns Images

Cover Photo by *Jupiter Images*/IFA Bilderteam/Mark Wunsch

The photographs in this book are used with permission and through the courtesy of:
Peter Arnold: pp. 1, 21 PHONE/Thiriet Claudius; p. 3 Alan Majchrowicz; p. 27 H. Reinhard.
Photo Researchers: p. 5 Hans Reinhard. *SuperStock*: pp. 7, 29L SuperStock; pp. 9, 28TR Photodisc;
pp. 17, 29R Sal Maimone. *Alamy Images*: pp. 11, 25, 28TL Arco Images; p. 15 David Rose;
pp. 19, 28BL Picture Partners. *Animals Animals*: pp. 13, 28BR G.I.Bernard/O.S.F.; p. 23 Lynn Stone.

Printed in Malaysia
1 3 5 6 4 2